LIFE THROUGH MY EYES

A COLLECTION OF POETRY AND PROSE

Other books by Rose Bingham:

Buy the Little Ones a Dolly (memoir)

Say It Isn't So and Then Make Lemonade

LIFE THROUGH MY EYES

A COLLECTION OF POETRY AND PROSE

ROSE BINGHAM

Henschel
H A U S
publishing, inc.
Milwaukee, Wisconsin

Published by
HenschelHAUS Publishing, Inc.
Milwaukee, Wisconsin
www.henschelHAUSbooks.com

ISBN: 978159598-934-5
LCCN: 2022946609

Printed in the United States

Thank you, life,
for all that inspires me.

TABLE OF CONTENTS

WRITING

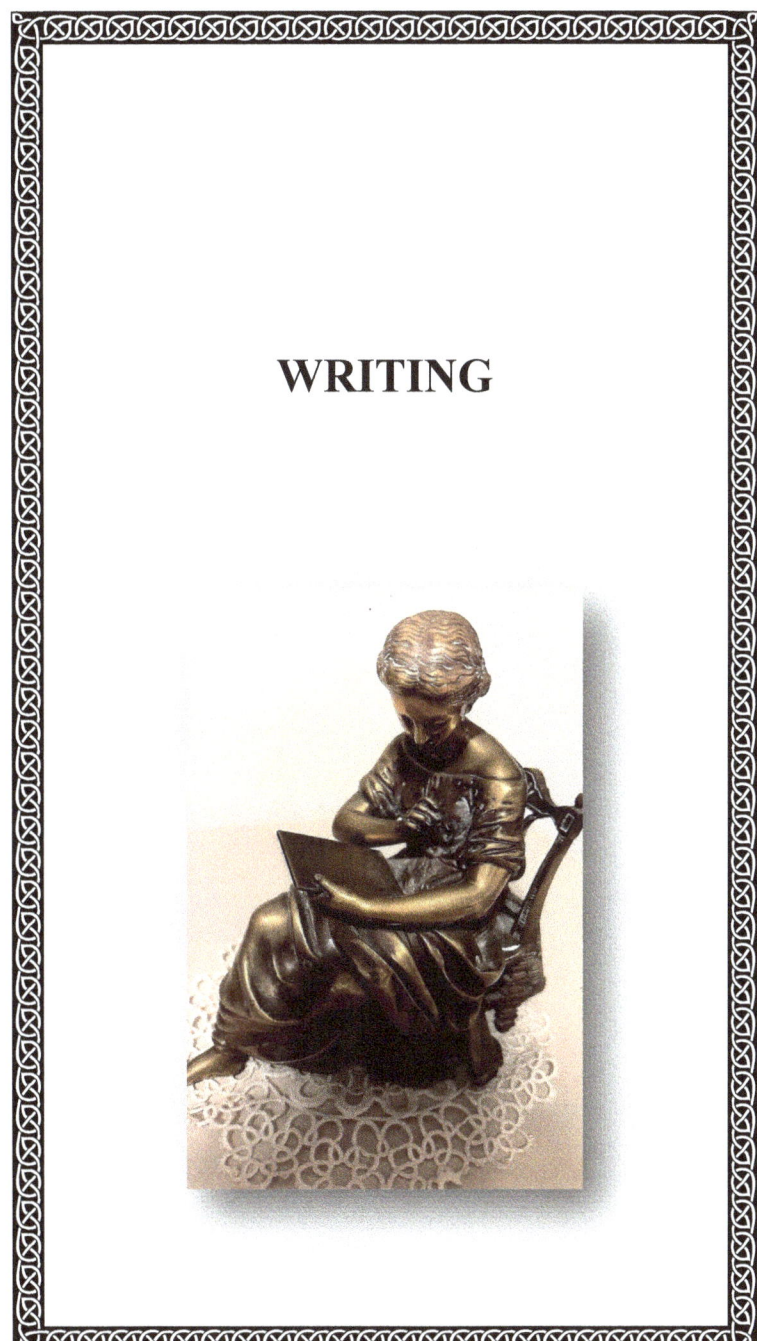

WRITING IS BEAUTIFUL

Why wouldn't one write?
We have reference material
right at our fingertips.

We have the alphabet,
twenty-six letters to do with
as we please.

We can create sadness,
happiness, surprise,
wonderment, mystery, and love.

We all have life experiences.
They are all different.
We can share them.

Walking outdoors is
like entering a library
with rows and rows
of subject matter.

We can write about a
crimson maple leaf
floating in a puddle, or of a
sunset with a palette of color
that takes your breath away.

Not all is happiness.
There is death lurking in the shadows;
abuse, drugs and alcohol—
subjects that need to be written about.

Pick up your pen and paper
and start writing.

SILENT HISTORIAN

A tree is a silent historian. As I look at a tree I often think how wonderful it would be if it could talk. I imagine the tree would tell me how it dug in its roots and hung on for dear life during storms. It would tell me about the insects and creatures of the forest. It would tell me of lover's secrets.

I remember looking up at a redwood tree in California, my neck and head practically resting on my shoulder blades in an attempt to visualize the top, and at the same time thinking what a story the redwood would tell.

I am fuel
I am paper
I am lumber
I am a scratch pad.
I am a umbrella
I am extended arms
I am a haven
I am a silent historian.

SEARCHING

I sit at my desk, my mind feels like an empty cave lined with cobwebs.

I am like a miner searching in the dark for a jewel hidden within dull walls of rock.

You see, I want my reader to see what I see, to feel what I feel.

Words on paper become like a mirror of oneself.

After all, where do ideas come from?

As bizarre as a poem or story may be, it is probably based on a life experience.

CHILDHOOD
MEMORIES

AUGUST 1945

I am eight years old; hair in pigtails, wearing bibbed overalls, and stretched out on a braided rug playing with paper dolls. Mom and Grandma are busy in the kitchen rolling out dough for fresh raspberry pies. The wood-stove is being tendered so the heat will be just right for baking the pies to perfection.

It is hot in the kitchen, and yet Mom and Grandma have full-length aprons on over their house dresses. Grandma has her hair pulled back in a bun, hairpins holding it in place. Mom's black hair frames her face, a strand making its way across her fore-head. Hands busy, she blows air upward, hoping the hair goes back in place. It never does.

Dad and Grandpa just came in from the field for a ladle of cold water.

The radio is playing. A booming voice is saying, "We interrupt this broadcast…"

Suddenly, everything stops in the kitchen. Mom, Dad, Grand-ma, and Grandpa are huddled around the radio. No one is saying a word. Grandma is still holding her rolling pin, hands cov-ered with flour.

They start hugging and twirling around. They look happy but they are crying. I don't understand. I ask Mom if they are sad.

She replies, "Oh no, we aren't sad. The war has ended."

Even at eight, I remember the day, but wouldn't understand the gravity of it all until I was older.

Rose Bingham

MEMORIES OF THE FARM

I am cuddled up under a feather-tick comforter, waking up
to the crowing of a rooster
and the smell of fresh baked bread.

I am a little girl in bib overalls,
hair in pigtails, walking into the barn,
watching kittens lapping milk, Holsteins swishing tails, and
horses gently snorting air
through their nostrils.

I am priming the water pump, hearing the squeak, squeak of the
handle, bending down and peering into the spout, delighted
when water appears, first a trickle and then a gush.

I am walking through the barnyard, listening to a chorus of pigs
oinking, chickens clucking, and cows mooing.

I am waving to Grampa who I see out in the field behind the
plow.

I am winding myself tight on my tire swing, lifting my feet off
the ground and spinning wildly.

I am strolling through the orchard anticipating the harvest of
apples and cherries.

I am walking past the front porch lined with lace curtains
drying on stretchers.

I am stopping to sit a moment at the edge of the pond, delighted
to see a goldfish peeking around a lily pad.

I am going into the cellar, a special place, with potatoes and carrots in the bins, sauerkraut curing in a crock, fruit jars on the shelf making a rainbow of color.

I am playing Chinese checkers with Grandma, the aroma of tea brewing on the potbelly stove, the end of a perfect day.

Rose Bingham

GOING TO THE FEED MILL

Clip clop, clip clop, clip clop
The rhythm of hooves upon the road.
Queenie happy for a day away from the farm,
as was my grandma.

Her favorite go-to-town hat
held in place with a hatpin,
The blue striped round glass
glistening in the sun.

Reins held comfortably in her weathered hands
Able to adjust speed, stops, and turns
with subtle movements of her wrists.
Years of practice.

I, sitting tall beside her,
wearing bibbed overalls
and a flour-sack-fabric blouse,
feeling special.

Soon we will be at the feed mill
The earthy smell of grain forever
etched in my memory.
A hefty man placing a bag of chicken feed
on the floor of the buggy.

And the best part of the day
going to the drugstore
for a chocolate ice cream cone.
A ten-cent treasure.

THRESHING DAY

Neighboring farmers and their wives arrived early to Grandma and Grandpa's farm, some in cars, some with horse and buggy; and the owner on a tractor towing the thresher. Several of the women brought their children. It was the practice of the area farmers to assist each other in the harvesting of the wheat.

The men gathered outside of the barn, waiting to set out to the wheat field. The women, already wearing their aprons, went into the house to help Grandma start preparing the food for lunch. Some were carrying pies with golden crusts, plump with apple, cherry, or mincemeat filling that they prepared the night before. As a child watching this, I could only hope there would be pie left by the time it was my turn to eat. I didn't watch for long as all of us children were ushered outside to play and not be underfoot.

When the men came in from the field, they would wash their hands in a basin set out by the back door. They would brush the chaff from their clothes.

The dining room table was a delight to behold. There were steaming bowls of mashed potatoes, squash, and gravy. Platters held roast pork. A bowl of purple cabbage gave color to the table. Applesauce made from the apples in Grandma and Grandpa's orchard was just waiting to be ladled onto someone's plate. There was an assortment of pickles on the relish tray: watermelon pickles, sweet, and dill pickles. There were breads and dinner rolls, all homemade. An assortment of pies was lined up on the sideboard waiting to be savored.

The men seated themselves at the table and said *Grace*. The best waitresses they probably would ever have, the womenfolk, served them. I don't know how they had the energy to return to the field after all they ate. The women ate next, and while they started doing the dishes, we children ate. There was always enough food.

At the end of the day, much gratitude was expressed, and plans were made for the next threshing assignment.

FAMILY

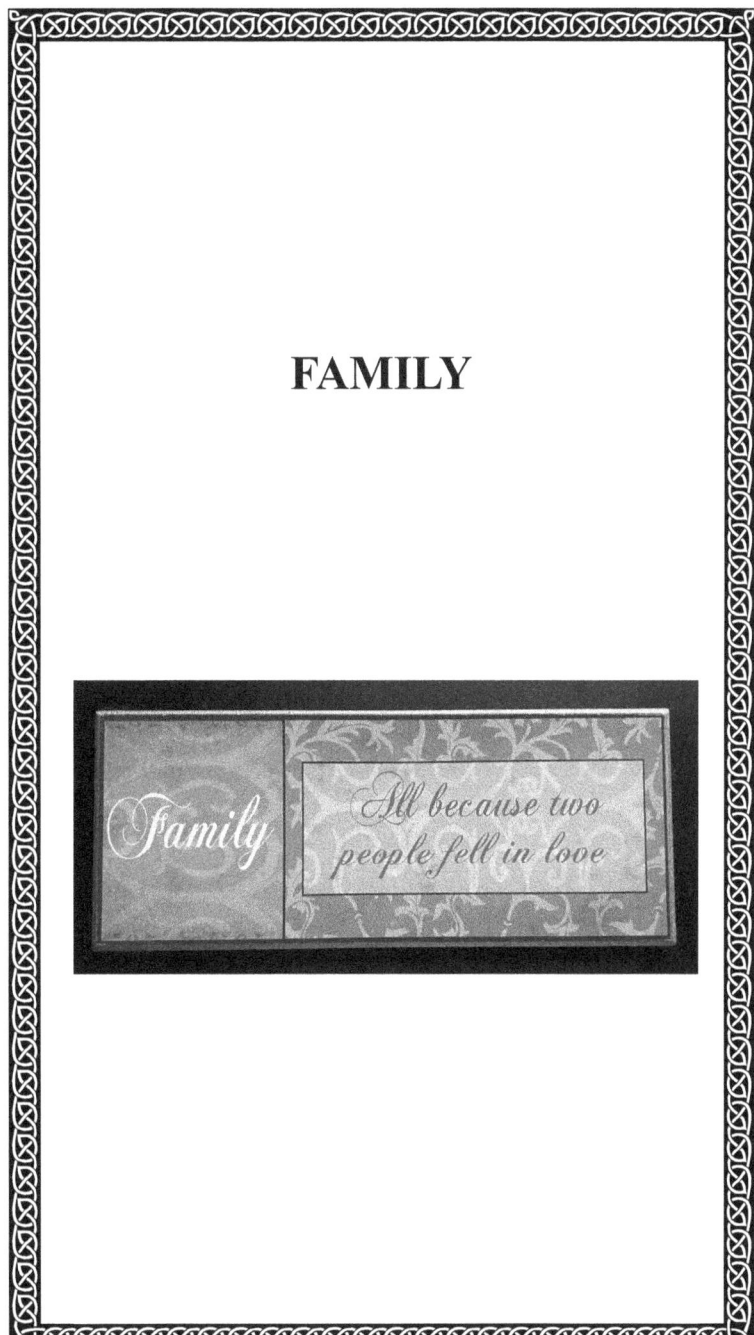

MY CHILDREN

I have raised them as flowers in a garden
Using tenderness when they were sprouts
Giving them guidance as they grew, but
Allowing freedom in their design
Fertilizing with care, love, discipline,
And values.
Six flowers in the same garden
But each flower unique.
Mike, who has the endurance of a
Sunflower and needs it.
Michelle, who dares
To be different, a rare orchid.
Julie, always
Dancing in the wind.
Mary, fragile and delicate as a rose,
Looking down at the
Caterpillars and ladybugs.
Mark, strong as a dandelion and such
A giving plant.
David, happy and busy as the bees
Who visit the garden.
You can plant a 100 seeds of the same variety
And yet no two flowers will be alike.
That is what makes gardens and families so
Beautiful.

~~Christmas 1983

JENNIFER, MY ROSEBUD

You are a tiny rosebud
Who will someday bloom
Into a beautiful rose
Your parents have had
A quarter century of
Blooming time.

Now they must protect you
From unnecessary harshness
And at the same time give you
The freedom to grow.

Your tears are the dewdrops, the
Color in your cheeks the delicate shading
Your lips the velvetness,
Your smile the uniqueness of you.

GRANDCHILD

What is a grandchild?
A gift from God sent to me
That is a grandchild.

Rose Bingham

YOU GOT THAT RIGHT!

My brother, the one who calls me 'sis'
My brother, the fisherman and hunter
My brother, the gardener, my fellow historian
My brother, whose favorite phrase is,
"You got that right!"
Do I love him?—
You got that right!

~April 2013

SISTERS

Sisters have a quiet
Bond that needs no
Explanation

A sister is one you can
Laugh with, cry with,
And share your deepest
Thoughts with

We have that, my
Sisters and I

~April 15, 1984

DISAPPEARANCE OF MOM
1952

LIKE DRIFTING SMOKE

Like drifting smoke
She was gone
I loved her so
She loved me
How could this be?

God had a plan
That I did not understand
Leaving me only with memories
Of a mother with a gentle face
And warm embrace.

The years went by
Was she safe, was she loved
Did she think of me?
I often cried, longing for my mother
With the gentle face
And warm embrace.

God answers prayers
In His own time, in His own way
His time was now
Sending a messenger
With a gentle face, a warm embrace

Filling in the pages
About a mother
With the same gentle face
And warm embrace.

Rose Bingham

I WISH FOR A MOMENT

I wish for a moment
I could go back in time
With my mother's hand
Tight on mine.

I would savor the warmth
of her touch,
The safeness I felt
A little thing that meant so much.

I would remember my first day of school
When she walked with me
Showing me the route I must take
And how to safely cross a street.

I would remember her gentle touch
As she fixed my hair
Sometimes in braids, sometimes in curls
But always with a loving touch.

I would remember walking in the woods
My hand in hers so tight
Stopping as she pointed out
Some of nature's delights.

I would remember the two of us on a sled
Her on the bottom, me on top
Arms wrapped around her
Until we came to a stop.

Yes, I wish for a moment
I could go back in time
Reliving memories
I can claim as mine.

THE SEASONS

Even the seasons form a
great circle in their changing,
and always come back again
to where they were.
~ Black Elk ~

SPRING OBSERVATIONS

Rivulets of rain
On the car window
Competing in a wild race.
(2013)

* * *

Leaves whispering
Flowers peeking
Birds singing
Winds blowing
Spring
(2013)

Rose Bingham

SUMMER JOYS

Echoes of a barn
Cows shuffling to their places
Metal stanchions closing
Milk rhythmically entering a bucket
Tails swatting flies
Kittens lapping milk
Echoes of a barn

* * *

Oh little firefly
Comforting me with your light
So small, so much might.

AUTUMN MUSES

Trees barren, silently
Mourning the end of summer
Empty nest syndrome.

* * *

Have you ever watched a group of turkeys?
Crossing a road, with determination in their step,
Heads aimed forward, like ladies rushing
To be the first at a garage sale?
All that is missing are their purses.

Rose Bingham

WINTER HAIKU

On a winter morn
Trees all decked out in crystal
Enhanced by the sun.

* * *

Shadows of oak trees
Sketched on a canvas of snow
Nature's art displayed.

* * *

Winter hanging on
Like barnacles clinging to
An abandoned ship.

NATURE'S REWARDS

A MORNING WALK

I walk at dawn and take in the great gifts of life, such as songbirds, fresh dew, green grass, spring rain, brisk air, sun, blue sky, clouds, plants, deer, a pond with frogs, scents, sounds, and my good health. It is soul food.

Peace comes like soft wind on my face. Love stirs. Hope calls. Will this day give me true joy, grief, smiles, tears, strength, friends, bad news, luck? Be glad, not sad.

Let us all work hard, play, trust, learn, teach, laugh, sing, have faith, pray, and give praise for that which warms our hearts. Thank you, life!

~August 2004

Rose Bingham

THE JOYS OF RAFTING

Rushing

Down

The

Rapids

In

A

White

Water

Raft

Exhilarating!!!

THE WORLD IS A STAGE

There is a curtain of rain,
A drum roll of thunder makes an announcement.
The rain exits; a backdrop of azure skies appear.

An accompaniment of birds gently chirp thanks
Frogs jump from puddle to puddle
Night-crawlers come to the surface much to the
robin's delight.

Nature's audience is treated to a freshness
in the air..
Evening comes
Lightening bugs flicker against the curtain of darkness.

Rose Bingham

MOONLIT GALLERY

Under a canopy of stars
accented by a half-moon,
I walk on a snow-covered road,
silhouetted by pines and oaks.

Nature has given me a ticket to her art gallery.
Trunks, limbs, and branches,
delicately sketched by nature's paintbrush
on a canvas of sky.

OUR DEAR PETS

Rainbow Bridge

"Just this side of heaven is a place called Rainbow Bridge. When an animal dies that has been especially close to someone here, that pet goes to Rainbow Bridge. There are meadows and hills for all of our special friends so they can run and play together. There is plenty of food, water and sunshine, and our friends are warm and comfortable.

All the animals who had been ill and old are restored to health and vigor. Those who were hurt or maimed are made whole and strong again, just as we remember them in our dreams of days and times gone by. The animals are happy and content, except for one small thing; they each miss someone very special to them, who had to be left behind.

They all run and play together, but the day comes when one suddenly stops and looks into the distance. His bright eyes are intent. His eager body quivers. Suddenly he begins to run from the group, flying over the green grass, his legs carrying him faster and faster.

You have been spotted, and when you and your special friend finally meet, you cling together in joyous reunion, never to be parted again. The happy kisses rain upon your face; your hands again caress the beloved head, and you look once more into the trusting eyes of your pet, so long gone from your life but never absent from your heart.

Then you cross Rainbow Bridge together...."

—Written by Paul C. Dahm

MIA

Walking elegantly into a room
Meowing ever so gently to announce her
    presence.
Slowly walking towards you
Brushing her body against your leg
Communicating with subtle movements
    of her tail.

Finding her spot in the room
Stopping to groom a moment.
Stretching, stretching, stretching
Rolling on her side and soulfully looking
    back at you.

Making eye contact with one of her toys
Pouncing on a favorite
Waiting for you to play her game
Rewarding you with a look and swish of
    her tail.

Suddenly stopping her play
Strutting back and forth in front of a recliner
Quickly claiming it as her own
Circling, snuggling, purring.

~December 2007

Rose Bingham

PRETTY BIRD

Pretty Bird, Pretty Bird
What a joy you have been
Not only a bird but a friend.

I loved watching you ringing your bell,
Waiting for me to say, "I'm going to get that bell."

Listening to your solo performances,
The best being your wolf whistle.

Appreciated your welcome chirp
The instant I would walk in the back door.

And then there was your commanding chirp:
2 PM—"Feed me."
8 PM:—"Put me to bed."

And my best memory is of you on football night,
Perched on the back of my recliner
Chirping as loud as I was cheering.

~Pretty Bird died February 5, 2008

MY RYLEE DOG

Born 01/01/2009
Bichon/King Charles Cavalier mix
Special gift in my life
A boy in a dog's body
Handsome
Smart
Gentle
Inquisitive
Friend to all
Loved Susie
Unconditional love
Gardening partner
Walking companion
Mind-reader
Lover of pillows and blankets
People greeter
Savored 'table' food
Nose like a detective
Favorite toys: bird, duck, squirrel, and puppy
Loved under the bed solitude
Disliked thunderstorms
Loved standing on arm of the recliner to
look out the window and watch the world go by
Rylee was special.

~Went to doggie heaven 05/11/2021

AUSTRALIA /
NEW ZEALAND

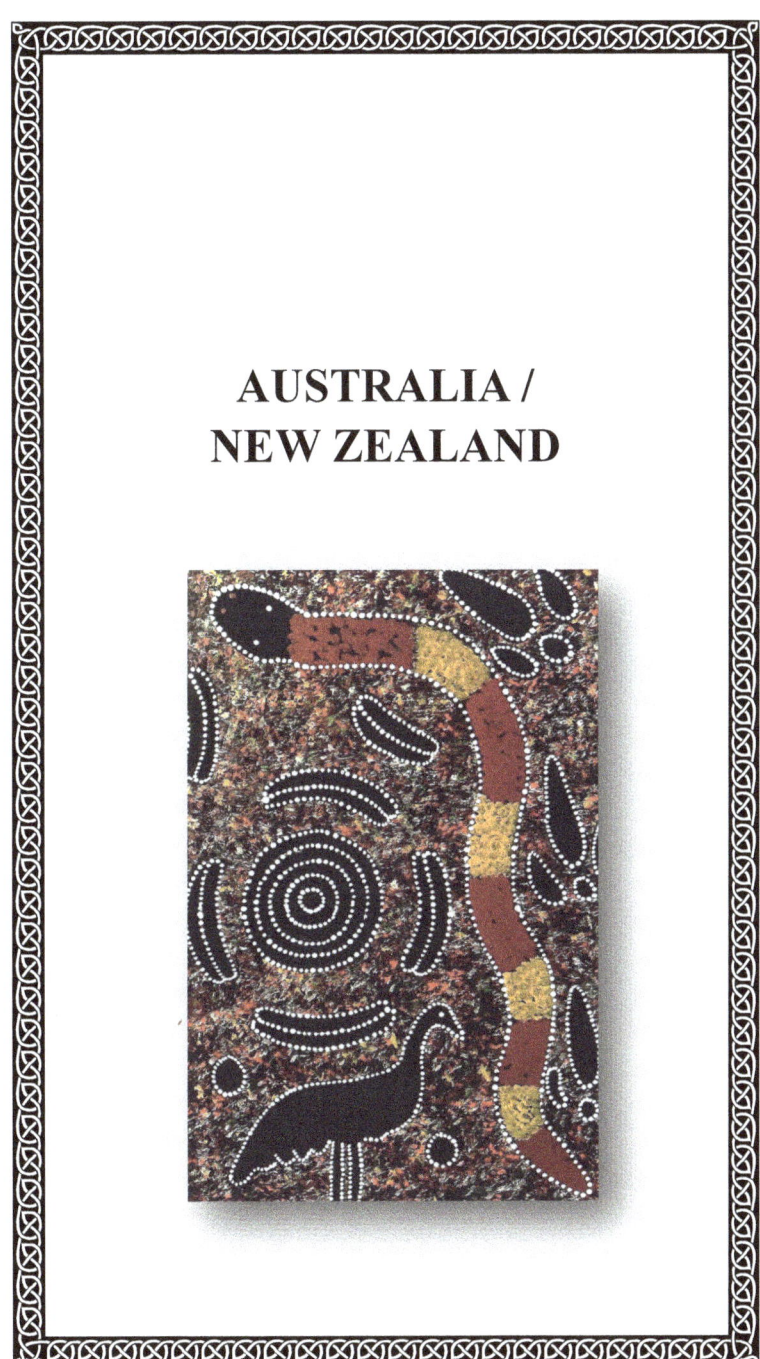

AUSTRALIA

I feel a serenity unlike any I have known.
Australia has a way of drawing you near
to hear and feel her heartbeat.

She wears a coat of many colors,
blue like the ocean,
green like the tropical forests and acres of fields,
orange like the desert,
white like the surf lapping against the rugged coastline,
multicolored like the coral reef,
tan like her millions of sheep, and shades of brown and gray,
like the kangaroos, camels, and emus.

Australia, you have captured my heart.
You have done this through your people, your land, and your
magnetism.

Your sunrises and sunsets have warmed my spirit.
Your vast skies have blanketed me.
Your stars have shown me the way.
The sounds of the didgeridoo have drawn me into your culture.
Your varied landscapes have stirred my emotions.
I will leave your land as a different person than when I came.

NEVER TOO OLD TO BUNGEE JUMP

This is an excerpt from my Australia/New Zealand travel journal. The date is September 26, 2001, and I am in Queenstown, New Zealand.

Today is a day filled with excitement and anticipation as I am determined to bungee jump.

I retired five months ago from a 43-year nursing career. Before we left on this trip of a lifetime, I consulted with one of the orthopedists where I had been employed, and said to him, "Is there any reason, being 64 years old, that I should not bungee jump?" I was thrilled to hear him reply, "If you're in good health, go for it."

So, here I am. We leave the hotel at 8:30 a.m. for Mt. Cook, with stops planned at an old mining community, and a bungee jump area. It is the practice on this tour after boarding the bus, for our tour guide, Ralph, to pass around a clipboard listing optional tours for the day. Today's optional tour is the chance to bungee jump. My husband, Mike, and I are sitting in the left front seat. I sign the sheet; my husband does not. The clipboard makes its way back to the front.

As Ralph is holding it, I notice my name is the only one listed. "Does this mean I can't jump?"

"This is your vacation. You can jump and the rest of us will be spectators."

We have an hour until we arrive at the site. I am feeling calm; no rapid heartbeat or sweaty palms.

We arrive at the Kawarau Suspension Bridge, the world's original bungee site. Ralph tells us A.J. Hackett Bungy restored the bridge. This 43-meter (142-feet) high bridge allows people, attached to a large rubber band at the ankles, to dive off and leap into oblivion.

We get off the bus. Several of the group is asking if I really want to do this. They appear more apprehensive than I. I go inside the building and spot the registration desk. They ask me my age. When they learn I'm older than 60, they tell me I only need to pay $20 instead of the $65 rate. I am entitled to a jump, photos, a video, a t-shirt, and a shot of brandy once I complete the jump. Although I'm not feeling nervous, I find I'm asking the age of the oldest person who has had this "wild ride." That brave soul was 92. Wow, I feel young!

I am led out of the building for a short walk to a covered area on the bridge. A friendly male New Zealander greets me with, "Howdy, mate." I introduce myself. I am asked to step on a scale. My weight is important for determining the length of the bungee cord. When I jump and the cord is extended to the maximum, he is asking if I want my head or fingertips to touch the water, or do I want to be a foot or so above the water?— Fingertips are good. He makes the necessary mathematical adjustments.

I am then asked to sit on a low bench with my legs out-stretched. A large Turkish towel, which has been folded in half, lengthwise, is centered beneath the calves of my legs. He rolls one edge of the towel toward the side of my left leg, leaving enough slack to place the rolled portion between my legs and repeats this on the right. Having me hold the rolled ends in place, he methodically winds a cord with a carabiner attached, up, over, under, and around the towel roll, and attaches it to the main bungee cord, which is about six inches across, and says, "A bungee cord is nothing more than thousands of rubber bands." Everything is secured with a large Velcro band. I am going to find out just how strong Velcro is—I hope. My thoughts are interrupted by, "Are you ready, mate?"

"Ready."

He takes my hand, helps me to standing, and I do a shuffle step to the door and onto a four or five foot gangplank. I hear cheering. My eyeglasses are off but I glance down and, through blurred vision, I see my fellow travelers on the observation deck. I wave. Although I'm wearing jeans, a tucked-in blouse, and a jacket, and because I'm a breast cancer survivor, I think to myself, 'I hope my breast prosthesis stays in place.'

I can make out the raft along the shore onto which I will be lowered after the jump, and the 150 stair-steps back to the top. The water shimmers below. The wind is brisk. The guide is telling me to let go of his hand, to think of a phrase that describes me at the moment, and then count 1-2-3 jump.

I can't find words for this moment. I only know I'm happy I'm here! I spread my arms and shout, "I'm a Sauk Prairie eagle. (Sauk Prairie is a town in Wisconsin where eagles winter.) One! Two! Three!—and simultaneously thinking, "If anything happens; what a way to go!"

The cord stretches out to its max I'm upside down My fingers touch the water The Velcro held I'm catapulted back up a ways It's not jerky it's smooth I see the sky I go down then up again I see the water I notice the cliff sides and shrubs growing out of them I hear cheers I love how this feels I'm slowing, stopping The raft is below me

The man on the raft is extending a long pole for me to grab onto. He says, "Relax. Get into a sitting position. Lower yourself to the thick foam mat. I manage, but rather clumsily.

He unhooks me, removes the paraphernalia, and assists me to the pier. My mouth is as dry as it has ever been, even "drier than cotton." Adrenalin, like an escalator is taking me up the 150 steps. My group is shouting words of praise. I go into the building. The staff presents me with photos, a video, and a t-shirt. I pass on the brandy. I don't want brandy to take away from what I just experienced.

When back on the bus, I am presented with a bungee jumping pin. I'm so thrilled I had this experience in New Zealand where it all began. My husband turns to me and says, "I'm thankful you were given photos and the video. I was so nervous; I forgot to aim the camcorder."

You are never too old!

WISDOM
&
REFLECTIONS

NO WASTED MOMENTS

Have you ever watched the
second hand clicking off time?
Time we cannot stop.
We must treat each second as a gem
No wasted moments.

Do you walk down the street
not looking at anyone,
your day's agenda filling your thoughts?
Take a second to greet a passer-by
No wasted moments.

Do you walk in the door and
start venting about work, the traffic…
Stop and ask your spouse, your children
How was your day?
No wasted moments.

Are you oblivious to the beauty around
A flower, raindrops on your face,
a sunset or sunrise?
Stop—take a mental photo
No wasted moments.

Are you glued to the TV, computer or I-phone?
Why not call a friend, visit a loved one,
take a nature walk.
Treat your time like a prized possession
No wasted moments.

Tick tock, tick tock, tick tock
Seconds on a clock
as precious as diamonds.
No wasted moments.

HANDS

If we look and listen,
Hands speak volumes.

A baby's hand,
small, velvety, fingers softly clenched,
which seems to say,
"I need someone to take care of me."

A child's hand,
maybe with a scrape or two covered
with a cartoon band-aid,
reaching up for the security of your hand.

A hand with rings on fingers,
bangles on wrists,
sparkle on nails,
making a statement.

Hands clutching a phone,
thumbs moving faster than the human eye,
making connections within their sphere.

Finely manicured nails.
What do they tell us?
Secretary, lawyer, model, writer, or
a woman who cares about her nails.

Hands reddened, rough, calloused,
strong and speak of toil and labor.
Construction worker, farmer, gardener?

Hands that have nurtured, soothed, prepared meals.
Hands that have clapped with joy
and wrung with worry.

Fragile, wrinkled skin,
gnarled fingers.
A hand that said I need you as an infant.
A hand that says
I still need you.

Rose Bingham

THE PALETTE OF LIFE

Ever changing, mirroring life's happenings,
reds for birth
green for child's play,
vibrant reds and yellows making
paths for teenage exploration.

White, a new palette for two people,
added color of pinks and blues,
pastels for peaceful times,
purple, black, and green for turbulent times.

The palette is full.
Grant me one more vibrant
brush stroke—my legacy.

WHAT IS BLACK?

What is black?
Black is night.
Is day better?
Without night, there is no day.

What is black?
Black is ebony.
Is ivory better?
Without ebony and ivory there
Is no piano.

What is black?
Soil is black.
Is green grass better?
Without soil, there is
No grass.

What is black?
Black is the color of skin.
Is white better?
Without our covering we
Are the same.

What is black?
It's just a color.

Rose Bingham

LESSONS LEARNED IN THE GARDEN

Kneeling down in my garden
I realize I am not alone.
There is a caterpillar on a mission.
I watch.

In undulating movements
he makes his way up a plant stem,
inch by inch, by inch.
I watch.

Crawling onto just the right leaf,
he waits, waits for his weight to
slowly lower him to a neighboring plant.
I watch.

He journeys down the stem.
His tiny feet like marching soldiers,
raising his head up so far,
he is almost erect, looking, looking.
I watch.

A wide blade of grass protruding
into the plant seems to beckon him,
stretching, stretching, almost
dangling in space, he reaches it.
I am in awe.

I glance at my watch. An hour has passed.
I am still on my knees, garden trowel in hand.
Patience, determination, perseverance,
Lessons learned in a garden.

(I am a breast cancer survivor. Gardening was therapy.)

YOU CAN BUY MY HOUSE
BUT NOT MY MEMORIES

I'm fortunate to have lived in a log home surrounded by stately pines, and oak trees whose limbs have been shaped by the wind, some leaning precariously but hanging on by the roots. Vehicle traffic is replaced with seasonal wildlife and a variety of birds.

Each time of the day brings its own agenda, but magic is felt in the early evening. I sit on my porch swing, close my eyes, and listen to the sounds of the night. I might hear the soothing, deep sound of an owl establishing his territory or maybe calling for a mate.

There are folks who find the repetitive call of the whip-poor-will annoying; I love their determination and never-give-up attitude. The call of the whip-poor-will is one of my earliest memories when visiting my grandparent's farm.

There is an awakening feeling in the Spring especially when the phoebe announces his/her presence: "Phoebe, Phoebe." I hear a wren claiming his territory—so little but full of confidence. Robins scamper across the lawn, looking for worms, a challenge in sand country. Baltimore orioles check out the feeder looking for oranges and grape jelly.

Not to be outdone by the birds are the hundreds of frogs who put on a symphony with a rich variety of mating calls.

On my strolls around the yard, I observed flowers emerge, unfold, and beautify the earth.

I heard the vibrations of hummingbirds' wings.

The calming sound of chimes on the front porch, orchestrated by gentle breezes, soothed my soul.

The twinkling light of the firefly, aka lightning bug, gave me the feeling of Christmas in July.

O little firefly
Comforting me with your light
So small, so much light.

Sounds of adventurous grandchildren echoed from the woods, "Grandma, Grampa, we made a fort from dead tree branches."

Just as parents tuck their little ones in at night, and themselves, birds do likewise. At first there is conversational chatter. I imagine they are saying it has been a good day; worms, bugs and birdseed have been plentiful, and no near misses. The chatter decreases in intensity and then you here gentle tweets, almost a lullaby, as they settle for the night, and then silence until the early morning wake-up call, the earliest risers being the phoebe and robin.

A well-used front porch filled with memories of family and friends, of conversations, some happy, some sad, holds a special place in my heart. Yes, you can, you can buy our house but not our memories.

Down-sized and moved from this home in August 2018)

LOSS

THE PINTO THAT REFUSED TO DIE

It was a lean year
Not much in the pocket
So we bought a used Pinto
Kindly called the "rust bucket."

Pavement you could see
Through cracks in the floor
But the Pinto's heart was strong
You could not ask for anything more.

But the day came
When those cracks in the floor
Became unsafe holes, so,
The car we could keep no more.

Our neighbor said,
"I'll take it!"
That Pinto's life
Is not done.

He drove it in a stock car race
You guessed it
The Pinto won.

Rose Bingham

THE VISIT

I take a number
I fill out a form
I place personal items in a locker
I take off my shoes and coat and put them in a container
The container and I pass through a scanner
My hand is stamped with invisible ink
A locked door unlocks
I'm out in the fresh air
Unwelcoming tips of barbed wire glisten in the sunlight
I wait for the iron gate to open
I walk through—the sound of its closure is chilling
My freedom is left behind
I enter a building
My stamped hand is scanned
I'm directed to a numbered table, a chair on each side
I anxiously wait
I see her, I stand up
We savor the one allowed hug
I wish she was back in the safety of my womb.

SAY IT ISN'T SO
AND THEN MAKE LEMONADE

A phone call
No, it can't be
Numbed to the core
A pain no narcotic could touch
A heart squeezed by the hand of grief
Please, I need to breathe.

So sudden
No time to say good-bye
Dear Lord
Help me to understand why.

Decisions, so many decisions
Obituary
Music
Readings
Pallbearers
Urn or casket?

Family, my source of strength
Friends, my source of healing
Faith, my source of peace
Powerful.

What I would give for
Just one more phone call
Just one more hug
Just one more, "I love you, Mom."
Good-bye, my beautiful daughters
You are gone but your spirit lives on.

Michelle 10/21/1960—11/28/2017
Mary   06/08/1963—02/03/2018

Rose Bingham

HEAVENLY TRAIN

I look up into the sky.
I see a widening vapor trail, but
I envision a heavenly train filled
with those who have gone before us,
taking an afternoon ride across the universe,
looking down at us trying to get our attention.

Are they happy with what they see?
Are they saying, "Good choice" when
they see their spouse's new partner?
Does the grandchild they never met,
look like them?

Are they telling us not to focus
on the color of our skin but on
the true colors of humanity?
Are they thinking will the
politicians ever get it right?

Are they pleading with us to
protect the environment?
Are they wishing they could
spend an hour with us?

I see a vapor trail, but
I imagine a heavenly train
filled with the wisdom.
of those who have gone before us.

WAR & UNREST

WHEN LIFE IS BAD ON BOTH SIDES

A man with tanned muscular arms,
waist cinched with a gun belt,
black, sturdy boots on his feet,
in sharp contrast with the white gloves on his hands.

A mother with dark hair,
wearing a bright blue tee,
denim jeans and blue tennis shoes,
her back to the man, arms extended,
hands placed flat against an official vehicle.

A child, no taller than a yardstick,
whose little face is framed by dark, curly hair,
looking cute in a red jacket, capris, and red shoes,
but with a look of horror on her face,
not understanding why the man is touching her mother.

She cries, but no one is listening,
except maybe the creatures of the desert.
She should be in a warm bed,
not standing in the dark illuminated by a blinding flashlight.

And then, another officer appears,
picks up the vulnerable,
struggling child and walks away.
The look of horror is now on the mother's face.

Rose Bingham

REFLECTIONS OF WAR

I am a quiet observer in a veteran's clinic.
I see men and women proudly wearing
caps, t-shirts, and leather jackets,
decorated with service-related patches
that announce, "I'm a vet."

Crew cuts, ponytails, long beards
define age and wars:
Korean, Vietnam, Desert Storm,
Iraq and Afghanistan, and maybe World War II.

Strong, healthy men and women
now with built-up shoes and prosthetics.
Some depending on others
to get from here to there.

I hear the hum of an electric wheelchair.
I hear the rhythmic cadence of cane tips striking the floor.
I hear resonant sounds coming from an artificial voice box.

I see a man with a scarred face with enough lip left
to make a one-sided smile.
I see a tall thin man walking at a snail's pace,
yet I feel his determination.

I see a distinguished-looking gentleman
wearing a dapper hat, and a suit tailored
to accommodate his amputated left leg.

I see a face with a blank stare.
Is he remembering,
or trying to forget?

I see vets greeting each other
with handshakes and warm hugs,
often sharing war stories.

I feel remorse for veteran's physical and emotional loss.
I feel appreciation for veteran's sacrifice.
I feel ambivalent toward war.

COVID-19

THE WORLD CHANGED
IN AN INSTANT—2020

Covid 19
Shelter in place
Wash your hands
Disinfectants
Safe distancing
14 day quarantine
Face masks
PPE's
Ventilators
Cases
Deaths
Ambulances
ER/ICU
Mortuary
Unsung heroes
Grief
Virtual hugs
Virtual Masses
Virtual broadcasting
Virtual weddings
No eating out
No sports
Unemployment
Food lines
96 cents per gallon gas
Stimulus checks
Zoom

Since we can't hit the delete button to get rid of this new vocabulary and virus, let's replace it with: HOPE, PATIENCE, VALUE OF THE LITTLE THINGS IN LIFE, FAMILY and FRIENDS (at a safe distance), APPRECIATING THE BEAUTY AROUND US, and PRAYER.

Rose Bingham

YESTERDAY

Yesterday I was free of spirit
Had freedom of mobility
Freedom to make decisions
Freedom to breathe, to touch, to hug.

Today an enemy lurks
in our world, doing
everything in its power
To bring us down.

I am 'sheltered in',
for how long is uncertain,
my fate determined by
scientists and doctors.

But wait. I am free.
Free to think
Free to write
Free to pray.

CLOSING
THOUGHTS

DUCK, DUCK, GOOSE

Death is powerful
as humanity stands
in a wide-ranging circle
playing Duck, Duck, Goose,
waiting for the tap on the shoulder.

There is no escape.
We can't quit the game.
Death is the decision-maker
who determines our destiny.

Death robbed a still-born baby,
the chance to meet the mother who
provided a safe haven
for nine months.

Death decides who
dies tragically and who
dies peacefully.
Is it fair he chooses
entire families at once?

Just maybe, maybe being chosen
is a privilege
beyond our imagination.
Are those standing the
unfortunate?

Whoosh, whoosh, whoosh.
Death determinedly
circles, circles, circles.
Duck, Duck, Goose.
I feel the tap.

Rose Bingham

COCOON

Oh, the warmth and safety of my cocoon
Protected me until I emerged
A butterfly, who knew not its destination,
Vulnerable in earthly vastness,
But what a wonderful flight, and now,
My color fading, wings tattered, I am
Spiraling toward the reward of a spiritual cocoon.

~ July 1, 1991

LIFE CLOCK

Slowly, so slowly
My life clock is winding down
Slowly, slowly, stop.

Thank you, dear reader, for viewing the world through my eyes.

ABOUT THE AUTHOR

Rose Bingham is a retired registered nurse. She graduated from St. Francis School of Nursing in LaCrosse, Wisconsin in 1958, and received her BSN from the University of Wisconsin in Madison in 1996. She enjoys writing poetry and has been recognized for such at the annual Writer's Conference in Madison, Wisconsin in 2013, 2014, and 2015, with one of the poems published in the Midwest Review 4, a literary and arts magazine published by the University of Wisconsin-Madison Division of Continuing Studies. Her memoir, *Buy The Little Ones A Dolly*, was published in December 2017 and *Say It Isn't So And Then Make Lemonade* in July 2019 by HenschelHAUS Publishing. Rose is proud of her status as mother, grandmother, and great-grandmother. Rose resides in Reedsburg, Wisconsin with her husband, Mike.

May angels always be with you on your life's journey

www.rosebingham.com

www.ingramcontent.com/pod-product-compliance
Lightning Source LLC
Chambersburg PA
CBHW041607240626
47164CB00009B/201